Disney
ANIMALS
The Essential Guide

GLENN DAKIN

Contents

"I'm gone, man, solid gone!"

"Let's show 'em, Dumbo
- power dive!"

"Why, Mr O'Malley,
you are amazing!"

Introduction

HI KIDS, JIMINY CRICKET HERE! I want you to meet a bunch of characters who are all heroes to me. "Heroes?" you may say. "All I can see is a bunch of goofy animals!" Well, that's just my point. You don't need giant muscles or a magic wand to be a real hero. You just need to find that something special inside you that keeps you going when life gets tough. That's exactly what these stars have done. Don't worry though – it's not all serious stuff. This gang are a bundle of laughs, too! Come along with me – I'm a great guide!

Jiminy Cricket

"Any time you need me, you know, just whistle!"

★ PONGO AND PERDITA ★
These proud parents foil
a vile villainess.
(see page 8)

★ THOMAS O'MALLEY ★
This alley cat becomes
a posh puss.
(see page 12)

★ DUMBO ★
A big-eared baby
becomes a star!
(see page 18)

★ BAMBI ★
A forest fawn grows
up the hard way.
(see page 22)

★ BALOO ★
This lazy loafer hides
a hero inside.
(see page 28)

★ SIMBA ★
The cute cub's rocky
road to royalty.
(see page 34)

★ MARL...
A w...

★ TIMON AND PUMBAA ★
The kooky couple who
hang out with a king!
(see page 38)

Mutts and Moggies

WATCH OUT – it's raining cats and dogs! These popular pets always seem to be in the thick of the action. Well, cats are too nosy to mind their own business and dogs are too stubborn to give up once they smell adventure!

Oliver keeps a lookout for trouble – and stray sausages!

Trusty

DYNAMIC DUO
Lady is lucky to have loyal friends like Trusty and Jock. This fearless duo risk life and limb to save Lady's true love, the Tramp, from being delivered to the dog pound.

LIVING RUFF
This mutt may look mean, but it's only daring Dodger. He's ready to defend abandoned kitten Oliver against all the dangers of life on the streets.

Jock

Meatballs make this spaghetti a discerning dog's top nosh

"Something tells me it's suppertime!"

PINOCCHIO'S PAL

Faithful Figaro will follow his master, Geppetto the toymaker, anywhere. They even journeyed into the stomach of a whale in search of their beloved Pinocchio.

NEVER-GIVE-UP PUPS!

Even mum and dad find it hard to remember all the dalmatian puppies' names – but you might recall little Lucky, ravenous Rolly and brave pup Patch.

"Just the same, Sergeant, use extreme caution."

WHEEL GOOD CHUMS

Napoleon and Lafayette just love chasing bikes and cars that pass their old windmill. And they especially enjoy biting the backsides of bad butlers who kidnap aristocats!

SOLDIERING ON

The Colonel always has his ear out for news, and Sergeant Tibs will brave any challenge for his old comrade, even entering Cruella De Vil's Hell Hall.

Tibs has learnt to stand to attention like a good soldier

KITTEN KABOODLE

Berlioz, Marie and Toulouse are Duchess's precious aristo-kittens. They are all tougher than they look! Marie reminds Berlioz that "ladies do not start fights, but they can finish them!"

Pongo and Perdita

DALMATIANS PONGO AND Perdita are parents to a horde of perky pups. The pair may appear pampered, but they will brave any danger for their family. Faced with Cruella De Vil, they go barking mad!

Pongo's "pet" Roger is a bit messy about the house, but otherwise well-trained.

Wealthy, wicked and wild about furs, Cruella De Vil has the peculiar idea that dog fur looks better on her than it does on dogs.

Unlike Pongo, Perdy has white ears

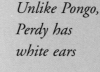

Perfect Match

Dalmatians Pongo and Perdita first met while Pongo was looking for a wife for Roger. Roger wrote songs about romance but really knew nothing about it at all — until Pongo arranged for Roger and Anita to fall in the same pond. Perdy and Pongo fell for each other at the same time!

Tired eyes from trying to sleep with wriggling puppies

Blue collar is a present from Anita

Puppy Boom

Pongo was looking forward to being a father, although 15 puppies isn't quite what he expected. Imagine having to remember all those names!

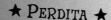

★ PONGO ★
- Pongo always acts like a perfect gentleman
- When he decides to stir Roger's dull life up a bit, he causes whatever mayhem is necessary!

★ PERDITA ★
- Perdita is a natural worrier, especially with Cruella around
- This quiet dog can turn into a wildcat when her pups are threatened

★ DOG LIKES ★
- Kanine Krunchies
- Strolling in Regent's Park in London
- Joining in the twilight bark – and waking half of London

★ DOG DISLIKES ★
- That "Devil Woman" – as they call Ms De Vil
- Roger playing his trumpet when it's afternoon nap-time

Roger managed to bring the last puppy of the litter back to life. After that, the pup was called "Lucky".

"Perdy, I'm afraid it's all up to us!"

Pongo's ears are alert

Black nose matches Pongo's black spots

The Dalmatians love to watch the adventures of Thunderbolt, heroic hound of the wild west. Little do they realize that their own lives are about to get just as exciting….

Name tag with Roger's phone number on the back

Dalmatian Doggedness

WHEN EVERY PUPPY PARENT'S worst nightmare happens, there's only one hope left – Pongo and Perdy are going to have to save the day all by themselves.

HOW TO SPOT A DALMATIAN
by Cruella De Vil

Lovely white fur – for my winter wardrobe!

Silly floppy ears

Stuck-up expression

Be careful – this end BITES

Spot the spots, you dummies!

REMEMBER! A Dalmatian's dark marks mean it's easily spotted.

Cruella hires crooks Horace and Jasper to steal the puppies. Things are about to get tough – for the villains!

Hopeless Horace is definitely not the brains of the team

🦴 Dognapped

When the pups disappear, Pongo and Perdy refuse to give up hope. Pongo recalls that dogs have a special way of sending messages in times of emergency....

Puppies have been heard inside Cruella's mansion, Hell Hall! The Colonel and Sergeant Tibs are on the case.

Jokey Jasper enjoys a merry quip while he's ransacking houses

🦴 Twilight Bark

"Fifteen spotted puppies stolen!" Pongo requests help by barking a message across London from dog to dog. And you thought dogs just liked being noisy!

The Longest Walk

Pongo and Perdy love their walkies, but this one takes the dog biscuit! It's an epic trek – even when you've got four feet instead of two.

1 Hell Hall – Pongo and Perdy rescue the pups and begin the journey to safety

2 Withermarsh – Towser and Lucy are ready to direct Pongo and Perdy to the Colonel

3 The Colonel and Sergeant Tibs's Suffolk farm

4 The Dalmatians use the stream to cover their tracks

5 The bridge – cunning canines hide on frozen stream

6 The dairy barn with milk on the house!

7 Pongo's shortcut to Dinsford is spotted by Cruella

8 Dinsford Smithy – the pups roll in the soot

9 Dinsford Village – where the Dalmatians catch the furniture van

10 Cruella heads for the bridge

11 Dog-tired, the pups escape in a furniture van

12 Horace and Jasper force Cruella off the road. Hurray!

A sooty disguise helps the pups to make it home and start a Dalmatian Plantation!

★ **Jiminy's Judgement** ★

Pongo and Perdita are spotty superstars! This dogged pair never give up. By rolling in the soot to hide their spots, they proved that animals are far cleverer than people!

11

Thomas O'Malley

KING OF THE ROAD, cat about town and all-round charmer, Thomas O'Malley is a natural romantic who just can't resist a damsel in distress – even if she is accompanied by three cheeky little kittens!

Madame Adelaide adores her pets. Her butler, Edgar, just pretends to like them – the old phoney!

"Oh boy, an alley cat!"

Duchess is an aristocat used to a life of caviar and cream – and so are her kittens, Toulouse, Berlioz and Marie.

Baddie Butler

When Edgar discovers that Madame's cats will inherit her money before he does, he plans to make them vanish. Four cats, each with nine lives – that's far too long to wait!

Stroll along the rooftops of Paris – and view this beautiful city as only a cat can….

Madame's mansion – home to the aristocats and Edgar!

The cats gulp down crème de la crème à la Edgar. This special drink is filled with sleeping pills!

"Keep your whiskers up, tiger!"

Fancy fur – Monsieur O'Malley may be poor but he always looks like a million francs

Well-groomed whiskers impress a lady cat

Tough Tom

Thomas is great at dishing out compliments and singing serenades but hidden underneath all that soppy stuff is a cool, streetwise survivor. The aristocats will be glad that they met this feline.

White tail-tip helps the kittens see him in the dark

The Eiffel Tower – handy for climbing up if there are dogs about

★ **FULL NAME** ★
(Take a deep breath)
Abraham deLacey Giuseppe
Casey Thomas O'Malley

★ **CHARACTER** ★
• Don't tell the others, but O'Malley *is* as nice as he seems
• This freewheeling feline is hoping to swap his bachelor pad for a family place

★ **LIKES** ★
• Flattering the pretty pussycats
• Outwitting hapless humans
• Jiving to jazz music with his pal Scat Cat

★ **DISLIKES** ★
• Being used for pitchfork practice
• Goofy geese teaching him to swim
• Being called a shifty philanderer (also by those geese)

O'Malley's Trail

EVEN A FUR-RAISING adventure can be a swinging time with this coolest of cats on your side. What's more, Thomas may finally prove to himself he's a cat and not a rat!

Magic Carpet

O'Malley boasts that he will rescue the Duchess on a magic carpet built for two. But when he sees the kittens, he chooses a milk truck. Hanging on the windscreen is a quick way to get a lift.

When Edgar dumps the pampered pussies in the wild, he thinks he'll never see them again. But then a lucky brown cat crosses their path....

★ SCAT CATS ★

This pack of jazz-crazy cats sure knows how to bring the house down. They also know how to bring down a baddie like Edgar.

Thomas's quiet, peaceful Penthouse – at least until Scat Cat shows up!

Le Petit Café – haunt of Uncle Waldo, the giddy goose

The windmill – home of those bike-chasing dogs Napoleon and Lafayette

It's in the Bag!

Edgar thinks his fortune is in the bag when he captures Duchess and her brood for the second time. But soon, he'll be the one getting the sack....

Thomas and Duchess enjoy a tender moment alone – well, except for three nosy kittens lapping up every word.

★ Always touch tails on a first date.

★ Out for dinner? Take your date to the classy dustbins.

★ Why watch a film when you can look at the Moon for free?

There's a nasty surprise in store for Edgar as he tries to pack the aristocats off to Timbuktu.

"We need a man around the house," decides Madame, as Thomas moves in – along with all the stray cats of Paris!

Thomas frees his friends and makes room for Edgar to take their place!

O'Malley shows his friends the high life

Notre Dame Cathedral has beautiful windows – and maybe a hunchback

★ Jiminy's Judgement ★

O'Malley is a real hero. For the sake of Duchess he is prepared to give up his easy life as a bachelor – for the even easier one of an aristocat!

Mini Marvels

Bluebirds fetch a fetching ribbon

These mice are super seamstresses

BEING SMALL IS NO problem when it comes to foiling baddies – in fact, it's great for getting under fiends' feet and cutting them down to size! Take a closer look at the little characters who make a big impact!

SEW HELPFUL!
Greedy Gus and jolly Jaq have two concerns in life: helping Cinderella and keeping out of Lucifer the cat's claws. This plucky pair, with a little help from a fairy godmother, make sure that Cinders *will* have a ball!

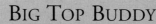

Gus   Jaq

BIG TOP BUDDY
Timothy Q Mouse brings jumbo-sized help and encouragement to Dumbo just when he needs it. He helped the elephant to rise from lowest on the bill to high-flying superstar.

Zazu stays slim so that Scar won't think he's worth eating

Stylish top hat is a gift from the Blue Fairy

PINOCCHIO'S PAL
If ever Pinocchio needs help he only has to whistle, and up pops Jiminy Cricket – chosen by the Blue Fairy to be the puppet's conscience. And Pinocchio will be sure to listen to him – sometimes!

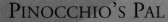

SENSIBLE SECRETARY
Even lion kings need advice sometimes, and Zazu is never slow to hand it out. One of his best suggestions was that Scar should be turned into a rug – so you could take him out and beat him!

Mice To See You

Timothy Q Mouse is Dumbo's best friend. He makes Dumbo realize that his big ears are an asset: "The very things that brought you down are going to carry you right up!"

Hiding under the hay is Dumbo's way of coping with stress, until he meets his pal Timothy.

Giant ears – ideal for catching thermals and gliding

★ **CHARACTER** ★
- Dumbo is gentle, shy and quite prone to bursting into tears
- He is a good listener. Well, with ears as large as those, he certainly ought to be!

★ **LIKES** ★
- A nice shower – from mum's trunk, of course
- Peanuts – he sucks them up like a vacuum cleaner

★ **DISLIKES** ★
- Clowns, cheeky kids and weird nightmares full of parading pink elephants!

Floppy ruff – marks Dumbo out as a clown

Lopsided hat issued by clown department to make Dumbo look silly

"Lots of people with big ears are famous!"

Timothy wears a bandsman's uniform as he is crazy about parades

19

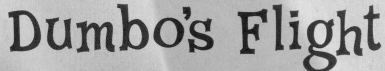

Dumbo's Flight

Dumbo will certainly remember his history-making, flying trip to fame. He soars through the air, believing it's thanks to his magic feather. But maybe this elephant doesn't need magic....

 ## Fall Guy

The clowns think elephants don't have any feelings at all and happily turn Dumbo into a laughing stock. The other elephants think Dumbo has brought shame on their species.

Tightrope – this high-wire act is finally upstaged!

Clown life is no joke for Dumbo. He is pushed off a burning tower into a tub of custard every night.

Giggles, Catty and Prissy love to natter!

After his circus show, Dumbo is shocked to wake up in a tree. Sharing the clowns' special water gave him an unexpected lift.

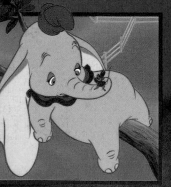

Grand entrance to the Big Top.

Roll up, roll up! Here's where the paying public queue to see the greatest show on Earth.

High-Flier

Dumbo dive-bombs the clowns and bombards his enemies with peanuts in his first display of elephant flying. Now, they'll all have to look up to him!

Clowns hide inside the burning tower, ready to push Dumbo out

This one's for mum! In mid-flight, Dumbo grabs the Mrs Jumbo disguise from the clown and sticks it on the ringmaster.

Dumbo learns he can fly without his magic feather

DAILY NEWS 5¢

UFO OR JUMBO?

AN UNUSUAL KIND OF JUMBO JET HAD THE TOWNSFOLK pinching themselves today, to see if they were dreaming. Maybe the opticians will be receiving mammoth orders for new specs, as people refused to believe their own eyes. Those who say that the pachyderm's pilot was a mouse are either very observant or very crazy.

Ear we go! Don't get in a flap – experts say it must be some wild circus stunt to sell tickets.

(story continued on page 3)

Life sure is different for Dumbo now that he's a flying star and he can share a luxury carriage with his doting mum!

Proud ringmaster – at last his show has a grand climax!

★ Jiminy's Judgement ★

It takes guts to rise above all the teasing and win everyone's respect. Dumbo proved that being soft-hearted doesn't have to make you a softy!

Animal cages for giraffes, tigers, gorillas, zebras and kangaroos

Clowns fire engine – not to be used in a real emergency!

Bambi

THIS FRAGILE FAWN is the gentlest, shyest creature in the forest. But soon he has to toughen up and face the hardships of the wild. Fetch a hanky – you may be crying a few tears before this section ends!

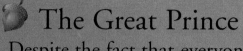 ## The Great Prince

Despite the fact that everyone calls Bambi "the little prince", it takes him quite a while to figure out that the Great Prince of the Forest is his father!

Bambi's dad gives him a kindly look when they first meet. It seems that stags don't go in for chat.

All the forest creatures come to take a sneaky peek at the baby Bambi. Well, it's nice to have someone to fawn over.

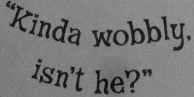

By accident, Bambi calls this skunk a flower, and he keeps the name. After all, skunks get called a lot worse.

"Kinda wobbly, isn't he?"

Thumper's thumping hind feet show his excitement

Jiminy's Cute-ometer

★ 45 55 65 ★
35   75
25   85
0   100

25 CUTE: Bambi cuddling up with his mum, when he's just been born.

55 VERY CUTE: Bambi learning to walk. Where *does* he put all those legs?

75 TOO CUTE: When Thumper's girlfriend strokes his ears and trills a love song to him. Seriously soppy!

100 CUTE OVERLOAD: All those baby birds singing in spring. No wonder the owl shouts, "Stop that racket!"

How Cute Can You Go?

Hi kids, I'm here to warn you of the dangerous levels of cuteness here! Older readers who don't like frolicking fawns and fluffy bunnies should look away for a few pages!

★ CHARACTER ★
- As a fawn, Bambi is curious, shy and gentle
- As a stag, Bambi is brave and noble – like dad!

★ LIKES ★
- Bunnies, butterflies and baby birds
- Hiding behind his mum when he's embarrassed
- Copying the grown-up stags prancing about

★ DISLIKES ★
- Ice skating with Thumper – too much teasing
- Forest fires – no roast venison!
- Hunters

Big ears can hear Thumper from across the forest

Tail fur grows darker as Bambi gets older

Oh, Dear!

Bambi is so wide-eyed, innocent and clumsy, even his best friends enjoy a good laugh at him. Will this delicate deer really grow into a strong stag? It's hard to believe!

Bambi's huge eyes broadcast all his feelings

Bambi practises his shaky standing style

It's not easy to look an upside-down possum in the eye, but Bambi tries to be courteous.

Bambi's Journey

BAMBI'S LIFE CHANGES forever when hunters arrive in the forest with their fire, hounds and… guns. This is where the story gets sad – so put on a brave face and read on!

Thumper may be a batty bunny but he's always there for Bambi to fall back on – or on top of!

Just dear friends? When pretty doe Faline first meets Bambi, she sends him head over hooves into a puddle.

🌰 Don't Look Back

Bambi's mother senses danger in the air. She saves Bambi's life by telling him to keep running and not to look back. But only Bambi makes it to safety.

It's the hunt to find winter food that leads Bambi's mother from the shelter of the woods into danger.

Bambi's only chance of escaping the hunters is to head for the forest edge where he can blend in with the trees.

A dramatic encounter on a bitter day in the dark forest begins to turn Bambi's fortunes around….

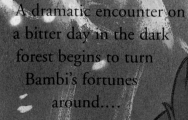

🌰 Stag Party

Life brightens up again for Bambi when Dad arrives on the scene. This mysterious loner suddenly pops out of the shadows and finally decides it's time to hang out with his son.

"Come, my son!"

Bambi didn't realise he could fight, until a rival tried to take Faline away.

When hounds corner Faline, Bambi sees them off, and shows that his antlers aren't just for decoration.

A campfire turns the forest into a roaring blaze. Bambi and dad hotfoot it out of there.

Life comes full circle for Bambi as he becomes a proud dad – to twins. Dear deer!

★ Jiminy's Judgement ★

Bambi started out life too scared to say hello to a doe. Getting over his tragic loss to become a legend of the forest is, well, staggering!

25

Wild and Crazy Guys

FROM THE INDIAN jungles to the African bush, these kooky characters roam free – just waiting for an adventure where they can live up to their reputation. Let's face it – these guys aren't called wild for nothing!

Squeezing lips creates horn impression

"I give the orders around here!"

RIGHT ROYAL RAVER
This self-styled King of the Swingers kidnaps Mowgli – at least it keeps the Man-cub away from Shere Khan for a while. Being a mere orang-utan makes King Louie go ape – he wants to be a man!

MARCHING MASTODON
Colonel Hathi is devoted to his son, but slightly scared of his wife, Winifred! He's always on patrol, marching his company of elephants across Africa. Why? Nobody seems to know!

Hathi's cane is ideal for pointing out sloppy haircuts and stray Man-cubs

TARZAN'S TOP TWO

Tomboy Terk and easily terrified Tantor will stick by Tarzan through any peril – even the arrival of that weird-looking ape, Jane! And if Terk the gorilla's in danger, Tantor never forgets to come to the rescue.

MYSTICAL MEDICINE MAN

Respected by the lions of Pride Rock, wise baboon Rafiki performs ritual ceremonies. He is very good at giving out advice, especially the kind Simba doesn't want to hear!

Rafiki's hand gesture represents the circle of life

BUMPTIOUS BEAR

When Kenai, an Inuit hunter, is turned into a bear, he needs more than a few tips on survival. Cool cub Koda is a bundle of attitude who becomes a true brother and lends a helping paw.

"I don't wanna brag or nothing, but I got some moves!"

MUMBLING MOOSE

Brothers Rutt and Tuke are natural comedians who love trading insults like "pinecone breath" and "crusty tail". They're always ready to offer guidance to bears in trouble, even if it doesn't always make sense!

FEATHERED FRIENDS

Buzzie, Flaps, Ziggy and Dizzy are soft-hearted scavengers, who help Mowgli when they could have been planning to eat him! They love harmonizing and teasing Shere Khan.

Antlers haven't seen a serious moose-fight in years

Baloo

Groovy swinger or lazy loafer? This upbeat bear is a bit of both. If there's a crazy party or a cool pool anywhere to be found, Baloo will be there, enjoying the bare necessities of life.

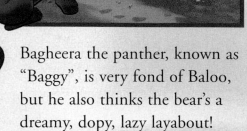

Bagheera the panther, known as "Baggy", is very fond of Baloo, but he also thinks the bear's a dreamy, dopy, lazy layabout!

Papa Bear

To Baloo the jungle is one big fun park – and when the Man-cub Mowgli comes along, he loves having someone to share it with. But being "Papa Bear" can be hard work too.

"You're gonna make one swell bear!"

Baloo's wild hair is as out of control as he is

Big nose can smell a ripe pawpaw across the jungle

Bear With Me

The only life that Baloo is an expert on is the easy life. Still, he decides to teach Mowgli everything that he knows. Bagheera figures *that* won't take very long!

Baloo knows that Mowgli must return to the Man-Village but he thinks that life will be bad for Mowgli: "They'll make a MAN out of him!"

★ **CHARACTER** ★
- A furry, fun-loving freeloader!
- Bone idle – he laughs at bees for working too hard

★ **LIKES** ★
- A good scratch
- Snacking on tasty, fancy ants
- Having nothing to do-be-do-be-do!

★ **DISLIKES** ★
- Flat-nosed, little-eyed, flaky creeps – in other words, mangy monkeys
- Holding a tiger tightly by its tail
- Being lectured by Bagheera the panther

Enormous stomach full of ants and prickly pears

Baloo shows off his boxing moves but he is easily beaten by Mowgli, who doesn't know that tickling is against the rules!

Fast feet for fancy dance moves

Baloo's tremendous tummy makes a great lilo for Mowgli to cruise down the river on.

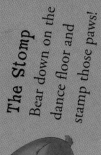

Funky Vulture
Wiggle your elbows and make like those batty birds.

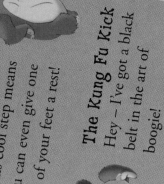

The Stomp
Bear down on the dance floor and stamp those paws!

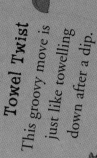

The Hop
This cool step means you can even give one of your feet a rest!

The Kung Fu Kick
Hey – I've got a black belt in the art of boogie!

Towel Twist
This groovy move is just like towelling down after a dip.

Tail Feather
Shake it, baby! Even if you haven't got a tail, it's wild to wiggle.

Baloo's World

BALOO JUST LOVES his big, beautiful back yard. But it's a jungle out there, and it takes special skills to survive. Whether it's finding food under a rock or bopping till you drop, here's Baloo's guide to jungle life.

Forest leaves are not just nice to look at – they're useful too. Especially for keeping your favourite little Man-cub warm at night.

Sightseeing

Don't let those pretty falls fool you – they are no place to take a shower! And don't bother with that tourist stuff when the best view in the jungle is a fat honeycomb hanging from a tree.

"Oh, man! This is really livin'!"

Itching to Have a Go....

When it comes to getting rid of a big itch, these knobbly old palm trees really come up to scratch. And the great thing is, if you find a tree that hits the spot, you can just pull it up and take it with you. If you're struggling, get a nearby bear to help you.

Just one tip – never ask a mean old tiger to scratch your back for you. They're sure to get the wrong idea!

★ BALOO'S SNACKING TIPS ★

Ants
Live under rocks and are kind of ticklish but go down a treat – if they don't crawl back up again. Just don't drop that rock!

Coconuts
What's so hard about opening coconuts? It's easy – I just crack them on my head.

Bananas
If they're too high up, get a strong pal to bend the whole tree down for you!

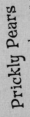

Prickly Pears
Claws are better than paws when it comes to picking tricky prickly pears. Save your poor paws for picking pawpaws.

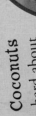

Baloo's Adventure

Baloo's life is a breeze until Mowgli turns it into a whirlwind of excitement. A trip to the ruins of an ancient temple is just the start of Baloo's attempts to save the Man-cub from peril....

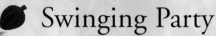 Swinging Party

Kooky orang-utan King Louie kidnaps Mowgli because he thinks the Man-cub can teach him how to make fire. Luckily, Baloo and Baggy crash the party and rescue Mowgli before there's too much monkey business!

Even when the temple is falling down, these dancers never miss a step

This ruined temple has stood for countless centuries – but it doesn't survive one single party with Baloo and King Louie!

"Give me back my Man-cub!" Baloo is too slow to stop the mad monkeys carrying Mowgli away.

"They ambushed me – thousands of 'em!" Let's hope Baloo's attempt to rescue Mowgli is better than his counting!

Louie thinks that owning an old throne is enough to make him a king

Multi-talented monkey

Snack stockpile for VIP guests

"Cousin" Mowgli enjoys the show

After fleeing the ruins, Baloo shows his true courage when he stops tiger Shere Khan from catching Mowgli.

Where He Belongs

It's a sad moment for Baloo when Mowgli arrives at the Man-Village. The Man-cub may be with his own kind at last, but he would sure have made a swell bear!

Baloo can handle tricky tigers and mean monkeys but when it comes to girls, he's plain terrified! Still, you can't blame Mowgli for being curious – after all, he's never seen one before.

Baggy describes Baloo as "one of nature's noblest creatures". The big bear's okay really – he's just loving the praise too much to get up.

Hollow logs make groovy drums

Crumbling ruins – about to get crumblier

Baloo's coconut disguise makes monkeys out of Louie's mob

Bagheera cunningly blends into the scene

The King of the Swingers struts his stuff

Whoops! Watch out for those banana skins

★ Jiminy's Judgement ★

Joker, loafer and serious snacker, Baloo shows that you don't have to behave like a hero to be one. When Mowgli needs him, Baloo can't bear to let his little buddy down!

Simba

Hᴇ'ꜱ ᴛʜᴇ ᴄᴜʙ who's destined to be king – but before Simba becomes top cat at Pride Rock, his evil Uncle Scar is going to give him a very rocky ride....

Even the day of his birth is no picnic for Simba as Rafiki pours melon juice over his head and shows him off to the crowds.

🐾 Top of the World

"Everything the light touches is our kingdom," Mufasa tells Simba. Sounds great, doesn't it? But what about the places where light doesn't reach? In the shadowy realm of Scar's hyena gang, dark plans are being hatched....

Mufasa tells Simba that there's more to being king than just doing what you like. You have to respect all animals – even those you eat!

Scar was in line to be king until Simba was born. Now he has to stand in line behind his nephew.

Royal Bulletin

I hereby proclaim that the future king, son of mighty Mufasa, shall be known as Simba and NOT "the little hairball", as Scar was heard to call him earlier. This did lead to some confusion.

Zazu

Advisor to the King

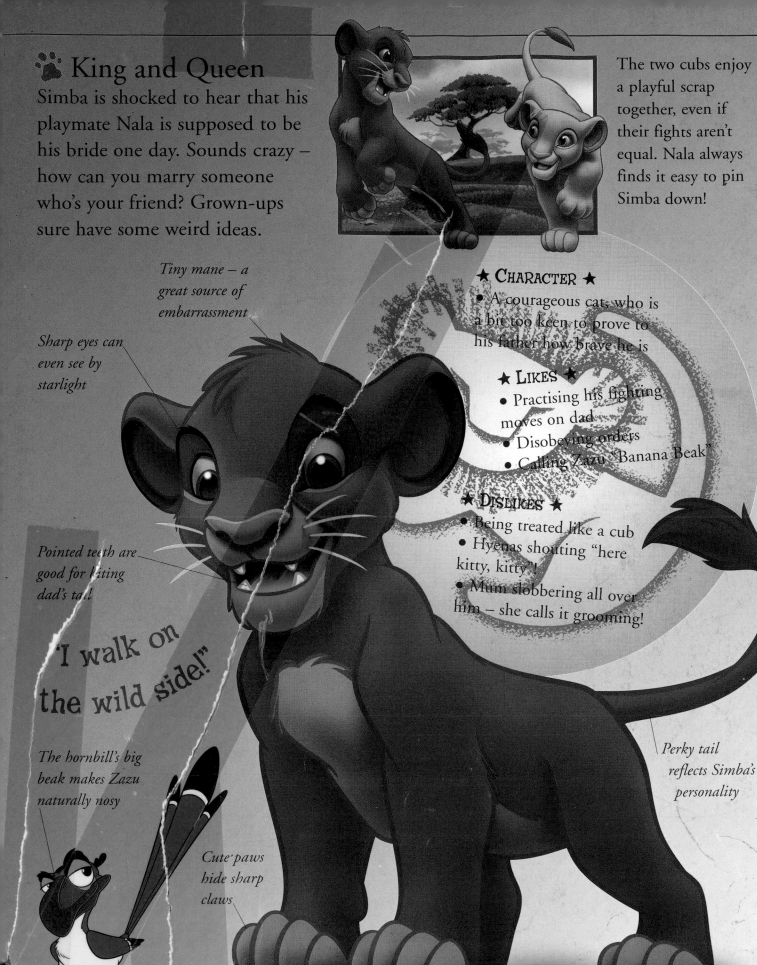

🐾 King and Queen

Simba is shocked to hear that his playmate Nala is supposed to be his bride one day. Sounds crazy – how can you marry someone who's your friend? Grown-ups sure have some weird ideas.

The two cubs enjoy a playful scrap together, even if their fights aren't equal. Nala always finds it easy to pin Simba down!

Tiny mane – a great source of embarrassment

Sharp eyes can even see by starlight

Pointed teeth are good for biting dad's tail

"I walk on the wild side!"

The hornbill's big beak makes Zazu naturally nosy

Cute paws hide sharp claws

★ **CHARACTER** ★
• A courageous cat, who is a bit too keen to prove to his father how brave he is

★ **LIKES** ★
• Practising his fighting moves on dad
• Disobeying orders
• Calling Zazu "Banana Beak"

★ **DISLIKES** ★
• Being treated like a cub
• Hyenas shouting "here kitty, kitty"!
• Mum slobbering all over him – she calls it grooming!

Perky tail reflects Simba's personality

Simba's Struggle

NO-ONE SAID THAT becoming king would be easy, but Simba's road to royalty is rougher than most. He has to face a great personal tragedy, and then he is tricked into taking the blame for it!

🐾 Beastly Shock

Scar leads Simba to a gorge and promises him a surprise "to die for". Scar knows that Simba will be in the path of the wildebeest. But it isn't Simba who perishes.

Simba has a grave experience in the elephants' graveyard when he meets the hyenas!

With his father dead, Simba flees the Kingdom. Even the hyenas wouldn't risk those prickly briars!

When Mufasa dies saving his son, Scar tries to blame the cub: "If it weren't for you, he'd still be alive!"

"He's so cute and all alone – can we keep him?"

Timon the meerkat and Pumbaa the warthog are delighted to discover exhausted Simba in the desert. An outcast, unloved, with nowhere to go – hey, he's just like them!

Simba always did look up to his father – now, he has to look up to the stars to see the spirit of his dad. Mufasa reminds him that he must take his rightful place. It's a "circle of life" thing.

When grown-up Simba meets Nala again, she brings bad news – and it isn't that she can still beat him in a fight....

🐾 Pride Restored

Scar has become king, and his evil ways have brought disaster to the Pride Lands. Simba decides that it is time to challenge Scar and face his regal destiny.

They say confession is good for you – well, it isn't for Scar. Simba forces his evil uncle to admit he killed Mufasa, and Scar loses everything.

No one can call Scar good for nothing – he actually makes a good snack for the hyenas after his final sneaky attack on Simba fails.

★ Jiminy's Judgement ★

Simba tried to hide from his sad past and forget about being king. But he realized that facing up to your problems is better than lion around doing nothing!

37

Timon and Pumbaa

N O RULES, NO RESPONSIBILITIES and no worries! That's the lifestyle that this crazy pair of pals enjoy until they save the life of a future king, and let him join their gang....

A New Start

Simba doesn't want to talk about his past when he first meets his new friends. That's great, as they don't want to hear about it!

Timon wants to flee from Simba, until Pumbaa points out that a friendly lion might be handy to have around.

Simba's new life is plain sailing – especially when it's Pumbaa's turn to be the surfboard.

Entertainment
Sometimes it gets dull saving kingdoms, so it kinda livens things up to dress up in a skirt and dance the hula.

Relaxation
Relaxing is no problem if you're a little guy – almost any jungle makes a comfy ha...

...our leg bugs ...instead!

...ition ...but so satisfying.

Don't Panic!
You must stay cool when you're in danger – running away and screaming is another useful tactic.

Being a lowlife doesn't have to be hard work. Here's the serious slacker's survival guide.

Just Lion Around

Hanging around with Timon and Pumbaa is just the tonic Simba needs to forget his woes. And he learns what it's like to look out for your friends, rather than just yourself.

The three pals spend a lot of time singing, mainly about Pumbaa's bodily aroma issues.

"Hakuna matata... no worries!"

Great vocal chords for singing harmonies with Pumbaa

Stylish shock of red hair

Tusks are handy for carrying fruit around on

Big snout for scenting juicy bugs

Giant lower jaw for delivering the perfect belch

Rumbling rump – steer well clear

When Simba has his battle with Scar, his pals trick the hyenas.

Despite the perils Simba's in, it's still pretty easy watching your friend fight for his life!

As Simba stares at the stars, he thinks the kings of the past look down on him. Timon finds that hilarious.

Watery Wonders

WHETHER PESTERING PIRATES, sabotaging sea witches or merely defying dentists, the ocean is full of creatures ready to lend a fin in times of trouble. So, why not drop in and meet the gang....

ARIEL'S ALLY

Fun-loving Flounder is the little mermaid's closest pal. Ariel tells him all the secrets she wouldn't want her dad to know – especially the one about falling in love with a human!

CRABBY CRONY

This crafty crustacean is sent to spy on Ariel, but he is such an unselfish shellfish, he ends up as her guardian angel. Sebastian's pet hate? French chefs with fish knives!

"Hop inside my mouth if you want to live!"

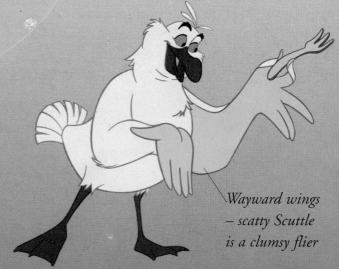

Wayward wings – scatty Scuttle is a clumsy flier

BIGMOUTH

It's not often a fish jumps into a seabird's beak and expects to get out again. However, Nigel the Pelican is only too pleased to offer Marlin a lift in search of Nemo.

GIDDY GULL

Ariel's friend Scuttle believes he's an expert on human life – although he does think a fork is called a dinglehopper, and that it's used for twirling your hair!

40

TANKS A LOT!

Pets or prisoners? These crazy captives help Nemo through a tough time when he is trapped in the dentist's aquarium. Nemo pays them back by proving that mad escape plans can succeed!

Peach

Bloat

Bubbles

Gurgle

Jacques

Deb

Ditzy Deb thinks she has a twin sister but it's just her reflection!

TICK TOCK CROC

Tic Toc once bit off Captain Hook's hand and now wants the rest of him! The croc swallowed the pirate's alarm clock too, and it's still ticking....

Loud ticking from stomach warns Hook

MARINE MASTERMIND

Gill is the leader of the tank gang. He immediately shows faith in Nemo, and believes the little clownfish can be a hero. Maybe it's because the two fish have something in common: one weak fin.

"We're ALL gonna escape!"

TURTLEY AWESOME

Crush is a cool turtle who loves to surf the ocean currents. Crush and his son Squirt are so blown away by Marlin's escape from the jellyfish that they call him "Jellyman". The shelled dudes help Marlin and Dory on their way to Sydney by giving them a lift.

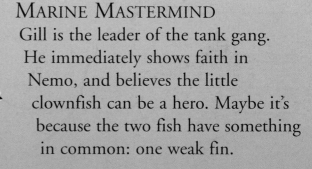

Marlin

LIFE ISN'T FUNNY for this clownfish – it's one worry after another! Since his wife and 400 eggs were snapped up by a barracuda, Marlin's been devoted to protecting his beloved son.

Marlin rescues Nemo from a tight spot – he's determined that nothing bad will happen to his son.

Letting Go

It's a fish-eat-fish world out there and Marlin is terrified of letting Nemo go on his first day at school. Marlin tells the teacher to watch over Nemo because one of his fins is rather small. That's one doting dad!

Is the coast clear? Then it's time to go – and watch out for charging sea snails! Marlin sure is a worrier!

Tail is like a mini-propeller, ideal for speeding away from hungry sharks

★ **CHARACTER** ★
• A kind, loving father, who will brave any danger to protect his son
• He can be *overprotective*, and needs to lighten up!

★ **DISLIKES** ★
• Anyone carrying a big net
• Dory's song – "just keep swimming". This silly tune gets stuck in Marlin's head

On a school trip, Nemo is caught by a diver. Marlin is distraught – he *must* find him!

★ **LIKES** ★
• Hiding safely in his cosy anemone
• Giving out safety tips and a constant stream of useless advice to Nemo

LISTEN TO DAD!

★ There's one key thing to remember about the sea – it's not safe!

★ Always look both ways before crossing a current

★ Never cuddle a jellyfish

★ Only hitch a ride in the beak of *friendly* pelicans

★ Unless you have a proper appointment, keep away from dentists!

Don't Forget Dory!

Marlin's luck changes when he bumps into Dory – she can help him find Nemo. She may be forgetful but Dory has many surprising skills, like reading human and speaking whale!

It takes Marlin a while to trust a flaky fish with short-term memory loss!

"Hey, Mr Grumpy Gills... just keep swimming!"

Marlin has three white stripes – good camouflage amongst anemones

Parental worry-lines on face

Relieved smile whenever he sees Nemo is safe

Marlin's Mission

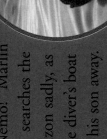

A LONG SEA TRIP might sound like a cool holiday to you and me – but to Marlin it's a desperate battle for survival, as he outwits some of the most dangerous denizens of the deep!

"Nemo!" Marlin searches the horizon sadly, as the diver's boat takes his son away.

"I've seen a boat!" Dizzy Dory points the quest in the right direction.

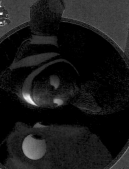

Follow the Trail…

Finding Nemo takes a bit of determined detective work, as one adventure after another leads Marlin and Dory closer to their goal. It began when Nemo touched the bottom of a diver's boat on his first school trip!

When the mask falls into the abyss, Marlin follows – and is nearly hooked by an anglerfish!

Fancy coming to a party? Bruce the shark takes them to the wrecked sub…

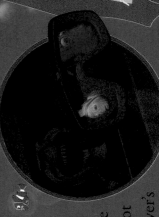

…where they spot the diver's mask. Time for a quick getaway!

Marlin's TOP 5 OCEAN ANGSTS

1. **SHARKS** – How can you trust a smile when it's made up of 3,000 teeth?

2. **ANGLERFISH** – If you see a friendly light, don't drop in for a bite!

3. **JELLYFISH** – They may look pretty but they're more than a trifle stingy.

4. **SEAGULLS** – That famous cry is just them calling "Mine! Mine! Mine! Mine!"

5. **HUMANS** – They think the ocean belongs to them and they don't even live in it!

"You've got serious thrill issues, dude. Awesome!"

Like, whoa, dude! Marlin rides the East Australian Current with the totally chilled-out turtles.

Dory tells Marlin not to touch the jellyfish. He ignores her and they are surrounded!

After Dory reads the address on the mask, the moonfish point the way to Sydney.

Superfish?

Marlin's heroic search for Nemo earns him the nickname "Superfish". Only Nemo can't believe it – tackling sharks? Nah, that can't be my dad!

Hitching a lift inside a whale forces Marlin to face the truth – he can trust Dory.

The finny friends end up in Sydney Harbour. Will they be a seagull snack?

Luckily the pair find a pelican crossing. Nigel the pelican crosses the harbour and saves them.

Brave Nemo escapes the dentist's surgery that he found himself in and bumps into dad near the sewage outflow.

★ Jiminy's Judgement ★

Marlin's bravest act wasn't facing sharks, but facing up to the fact that he wasn't letting Nemo live his own life. Hero Marlin proved that even dads can learn!

Together again!

And ready for new adventures....

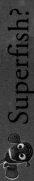

Beastly Beasts

Look OUT – there are bad guys about! As well as all the brave, big-hearted animals that are out there, some creatures are cruel and conniving, like this horde of horrors! Take a peek, if you dare – then run for your life!

"Everyone runs from Shere Khan!"

PESKY PET
Lucifer loves tormenting the poor mice at Cinderella's house. Don't let that smile fool you – he's even nastier than he looks!

TIGER TERROR
Man-cub is top of the menu for this cruel kitty, but luckily he ends up going hungry. Shere Khan may act cool, but he's a scaredy-cat when faced with fire – and he hates being called "Stripes".

Wrinkles form villainous scowl

HEINOUS HYENAS

These sinister, sniggering sneaks are Scar's horrible henchmen, Shenzi, Banzai and Ed. Their job is to do away with Simba, but it's usually the lion king that ends up laughing!

UNCOOL UNCLE

Most nephews enjoy the attention of their uncles, but Simba can do without the special treatment he gets from his Uncle Scar! This mangy-maned meanie is out to get rid of Simba so he can be king.

WRIGGLY ROTTERS

Flotsam and Jetsam are the putrid pets of Ursula the sea witch. These spies keep an eye out for little mermaids. Ursula adores the slimy stinkers and calls them her "poopsies".

TOY TRASHER

Scud loves toys – well, he loves to chew them and drool all over them. Luckily, Woody and Buzz Lightyear teach Scud and his master, Sid, a lesson.

Sharp eyes can spot helpless teddy bears

Piercing gaze on the lookout for unguarded baby's bottle

SI AND AM

These identical twin cats are exactly alike. They are both cruel, crafty and always in need of a snack – usually out of the family's fishbowl. Lady thinks they're purr-fectly dreadful!

DK

LONDON, NEW YORK, MUNICH,
MELBOURNE, AND DELHI

DESIGNER AND ART EDITOR Anne Sharples

PROJECT EDITOR Laura Gilbert

PUBLISHING MANAGER Simon Beecroft

BRAND MANAGER Lisa Lanzarini

CATEGORY PUBLISHER Alex Allan

DTP DESIGNER Hanna Ländin

PRODUCTION Rochelle Talary

ADDITIONAL ART Marco Colletti

"You mean the book's over already?
And the best-looking guys only get a
couple of pages? This stinks!"

First Published in Great Britain in 2006 by
Dorling Kindersley Limited
80 Strand, London WC2R 0RL
A Penguin Company
06 07 08 09 10 10 9 8 7 6 5 4 3 2 1

A CIP catalogue record for this book
is available from the British Library.

ISBN-13 978-1-40531-314-8   ISBN-10 1-4053-1314-5

Colour reproduction by
Media Development and Printing Ltd, UK
Printed and bound in China by Toppan

ACKNOWLEDGEMENTS
DK Publishing would like to thank: Lisa Gerstel, Graham Barnard
and Tishana Williams at Disney for their assistance;
Marco Colletti for his artworks.

Discover more at
www.dk.com